Let's Joke Around!

LET'S TELL JOKES ABOUT HORSES

Leonard Clasky

WINDMILL BOOKS

Published in 2023 by Windmill Books, an Imprint of Rosen Publishing
2544 Clinton St., Buffalo, NY 14224

Disclaimer: Portions of this work were originally authored by Maria Nelson and published as *Jokes and More About Horses*. All new material in this edition authored by Leonard Clasky.

Editor: Caitie McAneney
Book Design: Rachel Rising

Photo Credits: Cover Pavlina Trauskeova/Shutterstock.com; cover, pp. 1, 3-24 V_ctoria/Shutterstock.com; p. 4 anakondasp/Shutterstock.com; p. 5 (top) Bezkorovayny Dmitry/Shutterstock.com; p. 5 (bottom) Hussain Nalwala/Shutterstock.com; pp. 6, 8, 10, 12, 14, 16, 18, 20, 22 VectorShow/Shutterstock.com; p. 7 Kateryna Puchka/Shutterstock.com; p. 9 Sabrina Bracher/Shutterstock.com; p. 11 Konstantin Tronin/Shutterstock.com; p. 13 Alyson W. Kast/Shutterstock.com; p. 15 Anastasija Popova/Shutterstock.com; p. 17 gibleho/Shutterstock.com; p. 19 cornfield/Shutterstock.com; p. 21 Christy berry/Shutterstock.com.

Cataloging-in-Publication Data
Names:Clasky, Leonard.
Title: Let's tell jokes about horses / Leonard Clasky.
Description: New York : Windmill Books, 2023. | Series: Lets's Joke Around!| Includes glossary.
Identifiers: ISBN 9781538392911 (pbk.) | ISBN 9781538392928 (library bound) | ISBN 9781538392935 (ebook)
Subjects: LCSH: Horse, humor –Juvenile literature. | Jokes –Juvenile literature.
Classification: LCC PN6231.H59 C53 2023 | DDC 818/.602–dc23

Manufactured in the United States of America

CPSIA Compliance Information: Batch #CWWM23. For further information contact Rosen Publishing at 1-800-237-9932.

CONTENTS

HORSE DIVERSITY

Horses are amazing animals that have been around for nearly 55 million years. Many **species** existed long ago, but today there is only one species. With 400 different **breeds**, however, there is plenty of **diversity** in the horse world!

Baby horses are called foals. They can stand within a couple hours of being born. A young female horse is a filly, while a young male horse is a colt. Foals and young horses like to play around, just like kids. They're just *horsing* around!

THOROUGHBRED

HORSE BREEDS HAVE DIFFERENT SIZES, USES, AND **TEMPERAMENTS**. THE FASTEST HORSE BREEDS FOR RACING INCLUDE THOROUGHBRED, QUARTER HORSE, AND ARABIAN.

QUARTER HORSE

ARABIAN

HORSE TALK

HOW DO HORSES GREET EACH OTHER?

"Hay, neigh-bor!"

WHEN DOES A PONY SPEAK?

Whinny wants to!

WHAT DID THE PONY SAY WHEN IT BROKE THE STABLE DOOR?

"I was just horsing around!"

WHAT DID THE HORSE SAY WHEN IT FINISHED ITS BREAKFAST?

"That's the last straw!"

DIFFERENT BREEDS

WHAT KIND OF HORSE SWIMS UNDERWATER?
A sea horse.

WHAT DID THE HORSE BUY FROM THE BAKERY?
Thoroughbread.

WHAT'S AN ARTIST'S FAVORITE HORSE BREED?
A paint horse!

A GIRL'S MOTHER SAID, "YOU CAN'T HAVE A HORSE. THEY'RE TOO BIG!"

The girl said, "Well, what about a quarter horse?"

HORSE WORDPLAY

WHERE DOES A PONY GO WHEN IT'S HURT?
The horsepital.

WHY DID THE PONY GO TO THE DOCTOR?
Her throat felt hoarse.

WHAT KINDS OF STORIES DO SAD HORSES TELL?
Tales of whoa.

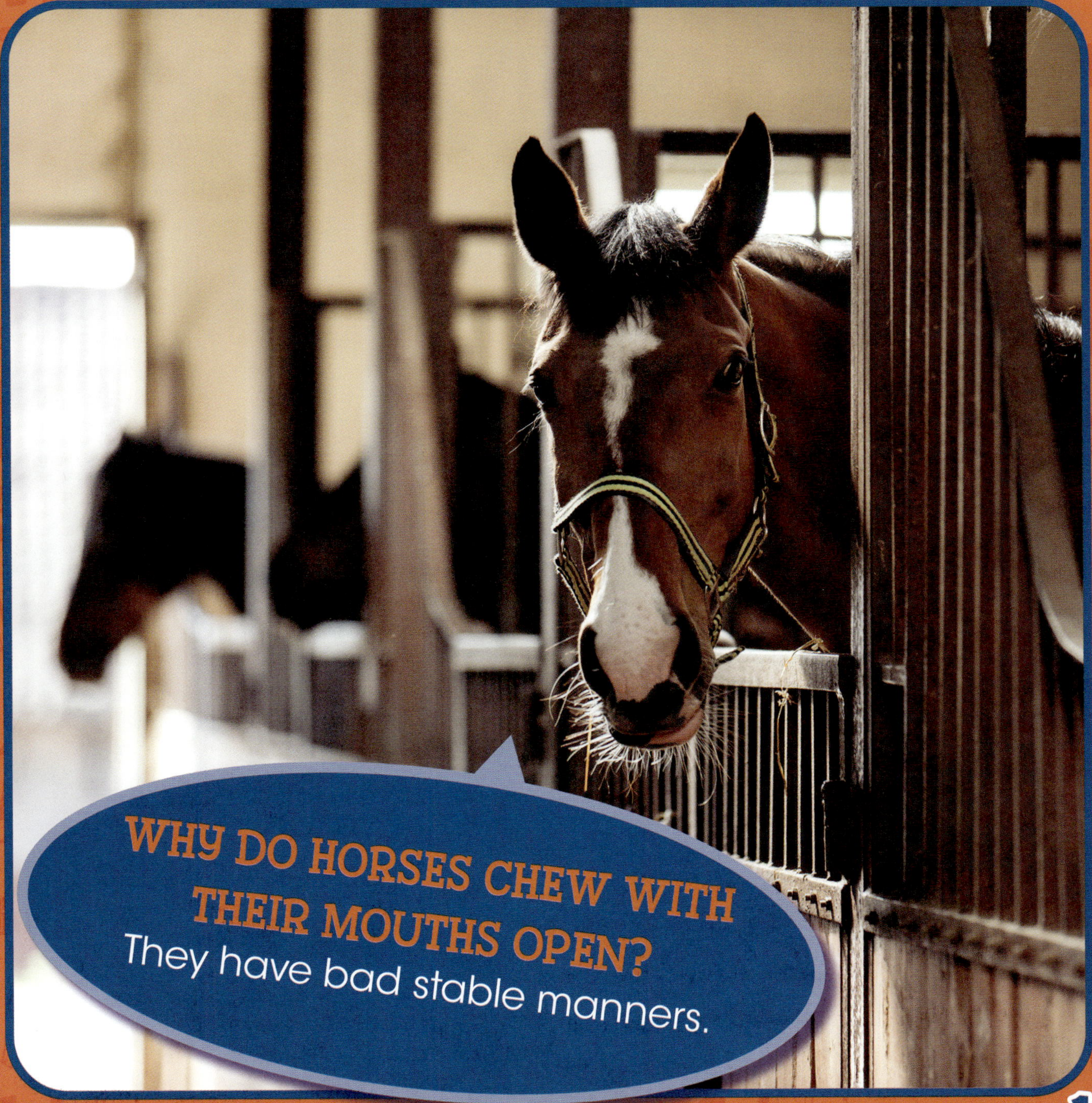

WHY DO HORSES CHEW WITH THEIR MOUTHS OPEN?

They have bad stable manners.

FOOD ON THE FARM

WHAT DID THE HORSE GROW IN HER GARDEN?

Horse radishes.

HOW DO HORSES STAY FIT?

They eat a stable diet.

WHY WOULDN'T THE MOTHER HORSE LET HER BABY SWIM AFTER DINNER?

You shouldn't swim on a foal stomach!

HOW DO YOU MAKE A HORSE SWEETER?
Feed it sugar cubes!

HORSE TROUBLE!

WHAT KIND OF HORSE CAN YOU RIDE IN YOUR SLEEP?
A night-mare.

HOW MUCH DOES IT TAKE TO FALL OFF A HORSE?
Just a buck.

WHAT DID THE MOTHER HORSE TELL HER SON WHEN HE STAYED OUT TOO LATE?
It's pasture bedtime!

WHAT DID THE HORSE SAY WHEN IT FELL?

"Help! I've fallen and I can't giddyup."

READY, SET, GO!

WHAT DO YOU FEED A RACEHORSE?
Fast food.

WHEN CAN A RACEHORSE GO AS FAST AS A TRAIN?
When it's on the train.

WHAT'S THE BEST PART OF A HORSE RACE FOR A VAMPIRE?
When it's neck and neck.

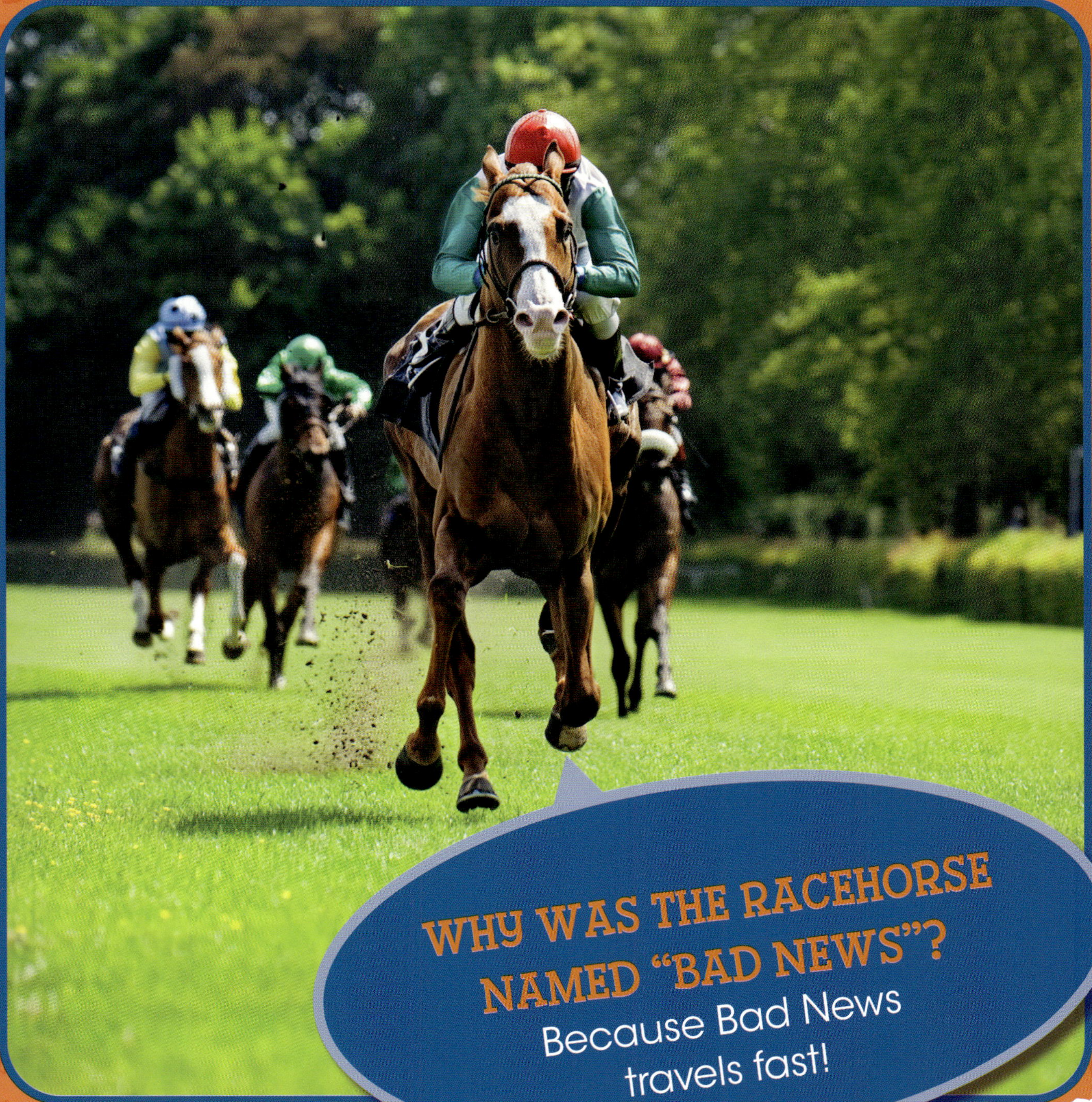

WHY WAS THE RACEHORSE NAMED "BAD NEWS"?

Because Bad News travels fast!

HORSE LOVE

WHO RODE A HORSE UP A HILL TO FETCH A PAIL OF WATER?

Jockey and Jill.

WHAT DID THE HORSE SAY TO HIS DATE FOR THE DANCE?

"Sorry, I have two left feet!"

WHAT DO YOU ASK A BROKENHEARTED HORSE?

"Why the long face?"

WHAT DO YOU DO BEFORE A HORSE GETS MARRIED?

Throw a **bridle** shower.

HORSES ON VACATION

WHAT DO YOU CALL A HORSE THAT'S TRAVELED THE WORLD?
A globe-trotter.

WHERE DO HORSES LIKE TO VACATION IN PENNSYLVANIA?
Philly.

WHAT'S THE FASTEST WAY TO SHIP A HORSE?
The Pony Express!

WILL THE HORSE GO TO THE FOOTBALL GAME?
Only if the Colts are playing!

FUN HORSE FACTS!

- Horses can sleep standing up. Their legs lock in position so they don't fall over.
- Some **ancient** horse breeds were smaller than dogs!
- Horse teeth take up more space in a horse's head than its brain. Still, horses are very smart animals!
- Horses can't burp or throw up. Their **digestive system** only goes in one way and out another!
- Przewalski's horses, native to Mongolia, are the only true wild horses on Earth today.

GLOSSARY

ancient: Having to do with something or someone from long ago.

breed: A group of animals that share features different from other groups of the same kind.

bridle: A set of straps used for controlling a horse that fit around its head and mouth.

digestive system: The parts of the body used to break down food.

diversity: The quality or state of having many different types, forms, or ideas.

jockey: Someone who rides a racehorse.

species: A group of plants or animals that are all of the same kind.

temperament: Nature.

FOR MORE INFORMATION

Books

Gottlieb, Beth. *I Love Horses!* New York, NY: Gareth Stevens Publishing, 2023.

Jeffries, Corina. *We Can Draw Horses.* New York, NY: Windmill Books, 2023.

Pang, Ursula. *Horse Farms.* New York, NY: PowerKids Press, 2023.

Websites

Przewalski's Horse
kids.nationalgeographic.com/animals/mammals/facts/przewalskis-horse
Discover the Przewalski's horse, the only wild horse breed in the world today.

10 Fun Facts About Horses
spca.bc.ca/news/fun-facts-about-horses/
Learn more fun facts about horses!

Publisher's note to educators and parents: Our editors have carefully reviewed these websites to ensure that they are suitable for students. Many websites change frequently, however, and we cannot guarantee that a site's future contents will continue to meet our high standards of quality and educational value. Be advised that students should be closely supervised whenever they access the internet.